Chefs' Special

Bengali Kitchen

Bengali Kitchen

Sujit Bose: Sous-Chef, Radisson Hotel, New Delhi

Lustre Press
Roli Books

Flavours of Bengal

West Bengal unfolds as a number of riverine tracts, fringed with palm trees and banana plantations. The mustard fields which carpet the landscape have given the state the name *Sonar Bangla* or Golden Bengal. Mustard itself is a necessary ingredient for cooking in Bengal.

Bengali cuisine is a combination of vegetarian and non-vegetarian food. Bengalis are on the whole an infectiously passionate lot and few things unite them more than their common passion for food-especially for fish. No meal is considered complete without it. Mustard oil, tempered with the five popularly used condiments (*panch phoran*) and the unique combination of fish cooked in yoghurt gives a distinct flavour to Bengali cuisine.

Rice and fish are the staple diet. A large variety of fish is available in the market. Different fish are eaten for different occasions: the *hilsa* is normally eaten between Saraswati and Kali Puja. The *topsey* is usually fried in batter and the *bekti* is filleted and fried or made with gravy. Other varieties of fish used include *pabda*, *rui*, *chingri* and *mourala*.

A lunchtime favourite is *sukhto* - served at the start of the meal. It consists of a mélange of diced and fried vegetables, some bitter (like bittergourd), some pungent (like white radish), some starchy (like potatoes), and some soft such as delicious stems and leaves which only Bengalis seem to eat. It is then followed by rice and *dal* (cooked pulses) accompanied by fried *bhajas* (cutlets) made out of vegetables and fish. There might be some *rui maacher jhal* (spicy fish curry). This is followed by a sweet and sour chutney and *aam jhal* (a watery soup made from green mangoes, flavoured with mustard seeds). Since Bengalis must have a sweet, there might be *mishti doi* - a thick, sweetened yoghurt set in earthen cups. Millions of sweets are consumed hourly in Bengal, the hot favourites being *rosogollas*, *sandesh* and *rasmalai*.

Rice and fish, other than being the main food items, are also used in Bengali customs. Rice is sprinkled over newly weds as a blessing; on expectant mothers and on boys during the thread ceremony. Crushed rice is used for doing filigree designs as decoration on festive occasions.

However Westernised, a Bengali would never give up his language; neither would he give up his Bengali food nor his passion for fish, rice and sweets. Most Bengalis do not touch salt-water fish, complaining that it lacks sweetness.

Bengali cooking brings a special art to the kitchen that is rare in any other form of regional cuisine and demands a little more care. Crisp, tangy, nutritious, spicy and wholesome — take 100 gm of adventurous spirit, deep-fry in 10 tbsp of enthusiasm, season with a pinch of experimentation and create your own Bengali gourmet delight!

Basic Preparations

Garam masala: 2 cloves (*laung*), 2 cardamoms (*elaichi*), 1 cinnamom (*dalchini*) stick, 1 bayleaf (*tej patta*), 5 black peppercorns (*sabut kali mirch*). Add these spices whole or else grind together to a fine powder. Sieve and then store in an airtight jar. For maximum flavour, make small quantities at a time, since it loses its aroma if kept for too long.

Mustard paste: Take 200 gm of mustard seeds (*sarson*) and wash well. Grind to a paste by adding just enough water to get a paste-like consistency.

Panch phoran: Mix equal quantities of fenugreek seeds (*methi dana*), cumin seeds (*jeera*), fennel seeds (*saunf*), mustard seeds (*sarson*) and onion seeds (*kalonji*). Store in any airtight jar and use as and when required.

Coconut milk: Grate the coconut and press through a muslin cloth to obtain the first (thick) extract. Boil the grated coconut with an equal quantity of water to obtain the second (thin) extract. If refrigerated, this can stay for up to 3-4 days.

Poppy seed paste: Wash the poppy seeds. Heat an equal amount of water and bring it to boil. Remove from the flame, add the poppy seeds and allow to soak for a few minutes. Remove and then grind to a paste on a grinding stone, using the minimum amount of water.

Channa **(cottage cheese):** For about 400 gm; boil 2 lt milk in a deep pot and remove from the fire. Add 160 ml vinegar or lemon juice till the milk curdles. Transfer the curdled milk into a muslin cloth to drain out the whey. Use either in crumbled form or else wrap in a muslin cloth and press down with a weight for half an hour or so. This will form into a block, which can then be cut to desired size pieces.

Dahi **(yoghurt):** Heat 1 lt milk till it is warm to touch. Add 1 tsp of yoghurt to it and stir well. Transfer to a clay pot, cover with a lid and then keep in a warm place to allow it to set. In winter it usually takes longer to set and also needs to be kept warmer than usual. In summer months, it sets in a relatively short time.

Doi Maach

Fish with yoghurt

Preparation time: 40 min.
Cooking time: 20 min.
Serves: 2-4

Ingredients:

Rohu fish fillets, washed	1 kg
Yoghurt (*dahi*)	1½ cups / 300 gm
Turmeric (*haldi*) powder	½ tsp / 3 gm
Clarified butter (*ghee*)	¼ cup / 50 gm
Cloves (*laung*)	2
Green cardamoms (*choti elaichi*)	2
Cinnamon (*dalchini*) stick	1
Bayleaf (*tej patta*)	1
Black peppercorns (*sabut kali mirch*)	5
Onions, chopped	½ cup / 100 gm
Ginger (*adrak*) paste	¼ cup / 50 gm
Red chilli (*lal mirch*) powder	1 tsp / 5 gm
Salt to taste	
Raisins (*kishmish*)	5½ tbsp / 80 gm

Method:

1. Marinate the fillets in half the yoghurt and turmeric powder for half an hour.
2. Heat the clarified butter and sauté the fish till it is three-fourths done. Keep aside.
3. To the clarified butter, add the cloves, green cardamoms, cinnamon, bayleaf and peppercorns. Sauté for a few seconds, then add the onions and ginger paste. Cook till the onions brown a little.
4. Add the remaining yoghurt, red chilli powder and enough water to cover the ingredients.
5. Return the fish to the pan and then simmer for atleast 15 minutes or until done.
6. Season with salt, add raisins and serve.

Lau Chingri
Shrimp with bottle gourd

Preparation time: 20 min.
Cooking time: 10 min.
Serves: 2-4

Ingredients:

Shrimps (*jhinga*), cleaned, deveined	50 gm
Bottle gourd (*lauki*), peeled	200 gm
Oil	4 tsp / 20 ml
Panch phoran (see p. 6)	1 tsp / 5 gm
Bayleaf (*tej patta*)	1
Ginger (*adrak*) paste	1 tsp / 5 gm
Red chilli (*lal mirch*) powder	1 tsp / 5 gm
Salt to taste	

Method:

1. Grate the bottle gourd, discarding the seeds.
2. Heat the oil in a wok (*kadhai*); sauté the *panch phoran* and bayleaf. Add the ginger paste and cook till it browns a little.
3. Add the bottle gourd and sauté till it becomes tender.
4. Add the shrimps and sauté over a high flame just for a few seconds.
5. Mix in the red chilli powder and 1 cup of water. Cook over a high flame till the liquid gets absorbed, stirring frequently. Serve hot.

Chingri Maacher Malai Curry

Prawns in coconut milk curry

Preparation time: 20 min.
Cooking time: 15 min.
Serves: 2-4

Ingredients:

Prawns (*jhinga*), shelled	900 gm
Turmeric (*haldi*) powder	3 tsp / 15 gm
Salt	3 tsp / 15 gm
Creamed coconut	½ cup / 100 gm
Water	3 cups / 600 ml
Oil	½ cup / 100 ml
Onion, large, chopped	1
Red chilli (*lal mirch*) powder	1 tsp / 5 gm
Sugar	1 tsp / 5 gm
Green chillies (*hari mirch*), chopped	3

Method:

1. Marinate the prawns with salt and turmeric powder. Keep aside for half an hour.
2. Blend together the creamed coconut and water. Keep aside.
3. Heat the oil in a wok (*kadhai*); fry the prawns over a high flame, until they are golden brown in colour. Remove with a slotted spoon and keep aside.
4. To the same oil, add the onions and fry till golden brown. Add the red chilli powder and cook for 2-3 minutes.
5. Add the coconut-milk mixture and bring to a boil .
6. Add the prawns and green chillies. Cover and cook over a low flame for 20 minutes or until the gravy thickens. Serve hot.

Potoler Dhorma
Stuffed Parwars

Preparation time: I hr.
Cooking time: I hr.
Serves: 2-4

Ingredients:

Parwars (*parmal*)	500 gm
For the onion-tomato gravy:	
Onions, chopped	800 gm
Coriander (*dhaniya*) powder	½ tsp / 3 gm
Cumin seed (*jeera*) powder	½ tsp / 3 gm
Turmeric (*haldi*) powder	½ tsp / 3 gm
Red chilli (*lal mirch*) powder	1 tsp / 5 gm
Ginger-garlic (*adrak-lasan*) paste	2 tsp / 10 gm
Tomatoes, chopped	150 gm
Salt	2 tsp / 10 gm
Water	1 cup / 200 ml
For the filling:	
Fish, deboned	250 gm
Oil	5 ½ tbsp / 80 ml
Ginger (*adrak*) paste	1 tbsp / 15 gm
Garlic (*lasan*) paste	2 tsp / 10 gm
Red chilli (*lal mirch*) powder	2 tsp / 10 gm
Salt	1 tbsp / 15 gm
Oil	¼ cup / 50 ml

Method:

1. Without peeling the parwars, scoop out the inner fleshy portion and blanch the shells in hot oil. Drain the excess oil and keep aside.
2. **For the onion-tomato gravy**, heat the oil and cook the onions till brown. Add all the dry spices, salt, the ginger-garlic paste and cook for 2 minutes.
3. Add the tomatoes and water; cook for 12-15 minutes, stirring continuously, till a smooth gravy is obtained. Remove from the flame.

4. **For the filling**, heat the oil in a pan; add the ginger and garlic pastes, red chilli powder, fish and salt. Cook for 10 minutes over a low flame.

5. Remove the pan from the flame; spoon the fish mixture inside the parwar shells.

6. When serving, place 1-2 stuffed shells in each serving dish, top them with the onion-tomato gravy and serve immediately.

≈

Fresher Fish
*To make refrigerated fish taste like fresh fish,
defrost the fish, add ½ tbsp salt and
juice of ½ lemon. Keep aside for
an hour. Rinse and cook.*

≈

Maach Bhaja
Fried Fish

Preparation time: 15 min.
Cooking time: 15 min.
Serves: 2-4

Ingredients:

Rohu fish, deboned, shredded	500 gm
Turmeric (*haldi*) powder	2 tbsp / 30 gm
Salt to taste	
Mustard (*sarson*) oil	1½ cups / 300 ml

Method:

1. Marinate the fish with the salt and turmeric powder for 10 minutes.
2. Heat the mustard oil in a flat pan; shallow-fry the fish till golden brown in colour. Serve hot.

Non-stick Fish
To prevent the fish from sticking while frying,
sprinkle a little water and lower the flame.

Saser Maach Kala Pata Dia

Fish wrapped in banana leaves

Preparation time: 20 min.
Cooking time: 10 min.
Serves: 2-4

Ingredients:

Rohu fish, cleaned	500 gm
Mustard (*sarson*) paste	
(see p. 6)	¼ cup / 50 gm
Salt	4 tsp / 20 gm
Turmeric (*haldi*) powder	1 tsp / 5 gm
Mustard (*sarson*) oil	4 tsp / 20 ml
Banana leaves (*kela patta*)	4

Method:

1. Mix together the mustard paste, salt and turmeric powder. Apply it over the fish pieces.
2. Brush 1 tsp of oil on each piece of fish and individually wrap in banana leaves.
3. Steam the wrapped fish either in an *idli* container or in a perforated container, put inside a large utensil with boiling water (one-third level). Cover the vessel and leave it over a low flame, so that when the water boils, it will steam the fish. Do this till the fish is done. Serve hot.

(Photograph on front cover)

Badha Kopi Maacher Muro

Cabbage with fish head

Preparation time: 30 min.
Cooking time: 40 min.
Serves: 2-4

Ingredients:

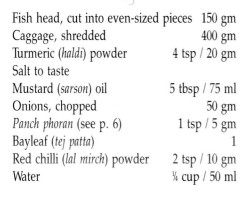

Fish head, cut into even-sized pieces	150 gm
Caggage, shredded	400 gm
Turmeric (*haldi*) powder	4 tsp / 20 gm
Salt to taste	
Mustard (*sarson*) oil	5 tbsp / 75 ml
Onions, chopped	50 gm
Panch phoran (see p. 6)	1 tsp / 5 gm
Bayleaf (*tej patta*)	1
Red chilli (*lal mirch*) powder	2 tsp / 10 gm
Water	¼ cup / 50 ml

Method:

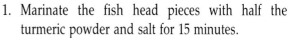

1. Marinate the fish head pieces with half the turmeric powder and salt for 15 minutes.
2. Heat the oil in a wok (*kadhai*); fry the marinated fish till golden brown and cooked. Drain the excess oil and keep aside.
3. In the same oil, sauté the onions for 2 minutes. Add the *panch phoran*, bayleaf and cabbage along with the red chilli powder, the remaining turmeric powder, salt and water.
4. Add the fried fish and cook till the cabbage is done and the water completely absorbed.
5. Serve hot.

Pabda Maacher Jhal
Fish curry

Preparation time: 15 min.
Cooking time: 30 min.
Serves: 2-4

Ingredients:

Pabda or pomfret fish	250 gm
Turmeric (*haldi*) powder	3 tsp / 15 gm
Salt	3 tsp / 15 gm
Mustard (*sarson*) oil	½ cup / 100 ml
Onion seeds (*kalonji*)	2 tsp / 10 gm
Water	4½ cups / 900 ml
Green chillies, slit	5
Green coriander (*hara dhaniya*)	2 tbsp / 30 gm

Method:

1. Marinate the fish with 1 tsp each of turmeric powder and salt for half an hour.
2. Heat the mustard oil and fry the whole fish till three-quarters done. Remove and drain the excess oil.
3. In the same oil, add the onion seeds, remaining turmeric powder, water and green chillies; bring to a boil.
4. Add the fish and cook for about 10 minutes. Serve hot, garnished with green coriander.

Maacher Chop
Fried fish dumplings

Preparation time: 45 min.
Cooking time: 15 min.
Serves: 2-4

Ingredients:

Rohu fish, boiled, deboned	250 gm
Potatoes, boiled, peeled	250 gm
Clarified butter (*ghee*)	1 tsp / 5 gm
Milk	1 tsp / 5 ml
Salt to taste	
Green chillies	2
Ginger (*adrak*) paste	1 tsp / 5 gm
Lime (*nimbu*) juice	1 tsp / 5 ml
Egg, white only, whisked	1
Breadcrumbs to coat	
Oil for frying	

Method:

1. Heat the clarified butter in a pan; add the fish, potatoes and milk.
2. Sauté for a few minutes, stirring continuously. Remove from the flame.
3. Add the salt, green chillies, ginger paste and the lime juice. Mix well.
4. Make small round balls of the mixture; dip it in the whisked egg white, roll in the breadcrumbs and then deep-fry until golden brown in colour. Serve hot.

Maacher Dim Bora
Fish dumplings

Preparation time: 40 min.
Cooking time: 10 min.
Serves: 2-4

Ingredients:

Rohu fish, deboned, shredded	300 gm
Onions, chopped	2 tbsp / 30 gm
Green chillies (*hari mirch*), chopped	2 tbsp / 30 gm
Salt to taste	
Red chilli (*lal mirch*) powder	2 tsp / 10 gm
Rice powder	¼ cup / 50 gm
Gram flour (*besan*)	¾ cup / 150 gm
Mustard (*sarson*) oil	½ cup / 100 ml

Method:

1. Mix the fish with the onions, green chillies, salt and red chilli powder.
2. Add the rice powder and gram flour; mix and let it stand for half an hour.
3. Divide the mixture into equal portions and shape each portion into flat round patties.
4. Heat the mustard oil in a flat pan; shallow-fry the patties till golden brown in colour. Serve hot.

Bagda Chingri Jhal
Lobster with mustard paste

Preparation time: 20 min.
Cooking time: 20 min.
Serves: 2-4

Ingredients:

Lobster, diced	300 gm
Mustard (*sarson*) oil	¼ cup / 50 ml
Green chillies (*hari mirch*), slit	5
Mustard (*sarson*) paste (see p. 6)	2 tbsp / 30 gm
Water	1 cup / 200 ml
Salt	2 tsp / 10 gm

Method:

1. Heat the oil in a pan; sauté the lobster for a few seconds and remove.
2. To the same oil, add the green chillies, mustard paste and the lobster.
3. Add the water and cook till the gravy thickens. Add salt and serve hot.

For Rust-free Knives...
Rubbing knife blades with vaseline and then rolling up the knives in brown paper, keeps them from rusting.

Mangsho Cutlet
Lamb cutlet

Preparation time: 1½ hr.
Cooking time: 20 min.
Serves: 2-4

Ingredients:

Lamb mince	500 gm
Bread slices	2
Garam masala powder (see p. 6)	½ tsp / 3 gm
Onion, finely chopped	1
Green chillies (*hari mirch*), finely chopped	4
Mint leaves (*pudina*)	1 tsp / 5 gm
Salt to taste	
Eggs, whisked	8
Breadcrumbs	½ cup / 100 gm
Coriander seeds (*sabut dhaniya*)	1 tsp / 5 gm
Clarified butter (*ghee*)	1¼ cups / 250 gm

Method:

1. Dip the bread slices in water, soaking them well. Remove and squeeze out all the water.
2. Mix together the lamb mince, bread slices, garam masala, onion, green chillies, mint leaves and salt. Keep aside for 1 hour.
3. Divide the mixture into 10 portions; shape each portion into flat cutlets. Keep them aside in a tray.
4. Add salt to the eggs and stir.
5. Heat the clarified butter in a wok (*kadhai*); dip the cutlets in the egg mixture, then roll in the breadcrumbs and fry until golden brown. Drain the excess oil and serve.

Mangsho Ghugni
Lamb with chick peas

Preparation time: I hr.
Cooking time: I hr.
Serves: 2-4

Lamb

Ingredients:

Lamb, boneless pieces	200 gm
Chick peas (*kabuli channe*)	½ cup / 100 gm
Oil	5½ tbsp / 80 ml
Onions, chopped	¼ cup / 50 gm
Ginger (*adrak*) paste	1 tsp / 5 gm
Garlic (*lasan*) paste	1 tsp / 5 gm
Tomatoes, chopped	¼ cup / 50 gm
Red chilli (*lal mirch*) powder	½ tsp / 3 gm
Coriander (*dhaniya*) powder	½ tsp / 3 gm
Cumin seed (*jeera*) powder	½ tsp / 3 gm
Water	1½ cups / 300 ml
Green coriander (*hara dhaniya*)	1 tsp / 5 gm

Method:

1. Soak the chick peas in water overnight; next morning boil till they are soft.
2. Heat the oil; add the onions, ginger and garlic pastes, tomatoes and the lamb pieces. Mix well.
3. Add all the dry spices and water; cook till the lamb is done.
4. Add the chick peas along with the water in which they were boiled. Let the mixture come to a boil. Remove from the flame and serve hot, garnished with green coriander.

Kosha Mangsho
Dry lamb curry

Preparation time: 45 min.
Cooking time: 1 hr.
Serves: 2-4

Ingredients:

Lamb (leg)	500 gm
Yoghurt (*dahi*)	¾ cup / 150 gm
Salt	3 tsp / 15 gm
Turmeric (*haldi*) powder	1 tsp / 5 gm
Clarified butter (*ghee*)	¾ cup / 150 gm
Onions, chopped	½ cup / 100 gm
Garam masala powder (see p. 6)	2 tsp / 10 gm
Ginger (*adrak*) paste	4 tsp / 20 gm
Garlic (*lasan*) paste	4 tsp / 20 gm
Coriander (*dhaniya*) powder	4 tsp / 20 gm
Cumin seed (*jeera*) powder	3 tsp / 15 gm
Red chilli (*lal mirch*) powder	2 tsp / 10 gm
Tomatoes, chopped	4 tbsp / 60 gm

Method:

1. Marinate the lamb with yoghurt, salt and ½ tsp of turmeric powder for 30 minutes.
2. Heat the clarified butter in a wok (*kadhai*); add the onions and garam masala powder (keep ½ tsp aside for garnishing). Cook for 10 minutes.
3. Add the marinated lamb. Cook for 10-12 minutes.
4. Add the ginger and garlic pastes, coriander powder, cumin seed powder, red chilli powder, the remaining turmeric powder and tomatoes. Cover and simmer till the lamb is tender.
5. Serve hot, with ½ tsp garam masala powder sprinkled on top.

Murgi Jhol
Chicken stew

Preparation time: 30 min.
Cooking time: 45 min.
Serves: 2-4

Ingredients:

Chicken, cut into 8 pieces	1
Oil	4 tbsp / 60 ml
Panch phoran (see p. 6)	2 tsp / 10 gm
Bayleaf (*tej patta*)	1
Ginger (*adrak*) paste	1 tsp / 5 gm
Garlic (*lasan*) paste	1 tsp / 5 gm
Tomatoes, cut into slices	½ cup / 100 gm
Turmeric (*haldi*) powder	1 tbsp / 15 gm
Coriander (*dhaniya*) powder	1 tsp / 5 gm
Cumin seed (*jeera*) powder	2 tsp / 10 gm
Water	2 ½ cups / 500 ml
Potatoes, cut into wedges	2
Cauliflower, cut into florets	2

Method:

1. Heat the oil; add the chicken and sauté for 1-2 minutes. Remove with a slotted spoon and keep aside.
2. To the same oil, add the *panch phoran* and bayleaf. Sauté for a few seconds.
3. Add the ginger and garlic pastes, tomatoes and the dry spices. Sauté further for a few seconds.
4. Add the chicken pieces and the water, followed by potatoes and cauliflower.
5. Bring the mixture to a boil; leave to simmer for at least half an hour or until the chicken is fully tender.

Murgi Kalia
Chicken curry

Preparation time: 30 min.
Cooking time: 15 min.
Serves: 2-4

Ingredients:

Chicken, cut into 8 pieces	1
Clarified butter (*ghee*)	¼ cup / 50 gm
Onions, chopped	1½ cups / 300 gm
Ginger (*adrak*) paste	1 tsp / 5 gm
Garlic (*lasan*) paste	1 tsp / 5 gm
Cloves (*laung*)	2
Black cardamoms (*bari elaichi*)	2
Cinnamon (*dalchini*) powder	½ tsp / 3 gm
Tomatoes, chopped	1 cup / 200 gm
Coriander (*dhaniya*) powder	1 tsp / 5 gm
Turmeric (*haldi*) powder	1 tsp / 5 gm
Red chilli (*lal mirch*) powder	2 tsp / 10 gm
Water	1 cup / 200 ml

Method:

1. Heat the clarified butter in a heavy-bottomed pan; add the onion and sauté until it becomes transluscent.
2. Add the ginger and garlic pastes, the cloves, black cardamoms and cinnamon powder. Sauté for a few seconds or until the pastes changes colour.
3. Add the chicken and sauté for 10-12 minutes.
4. Stir in the tomatoes, coriander powder, turmeric powder, red chilli powder and water. Cook till the chicken becomes tender and the gravy thickens.
5. Serve hot.

Aloo Chorchori
Potato delight

Preparation time: 15 min.
Cooking time: 30 min.
Serves: 2-4

V e g e t a r i a n

Ingredients:

Potatoes, thinly sliced	200 gm
Onions, thinly sliced	½ cup / 100 gm
Oil	2 tbsp / 30 ml
Turmeric (*haldi*) powder	1 tsp / 5 gm
Salt to taste	
Red chilli (*lal mirch*) powder	2 tsp / 10 gm
Water	½ cup / 100 ml

Method:

1. Heat the oil in a wok (*kadhai*); add the onions and sauté till light pink in colour.
2. Add the potatoes and sauté for 3-4 minutes.
3. Add the turmeric powder, salt, red chilli powder and water.
4. Cook over a medium flame till the potatoes are done and the liquid absorbed. Serve hot.

Aloo Bhata

Mustard-flavoured mashed potatoes

Preparation time: 40 min.
Cooking time: 5 min.
Serves: 2-4

Ingredients:

Potatoes, whole, boiled	300 gm
Salt to taste	
Green chillies (*hari mirch*), chopped	2 tsp / 10 gm
Mustard (*sarson*) oil	1 tbsp / 15 ml

Method:

1. Peel the potatoes while still hot.
2. Mash the potatoes; add salt, green chillies and mustard oil.
3. Take the potato mixture and shape into small balls. Serve with steamed rice.

Potato Perfect !

Cut potato chips will not stick to each other and turn out crisper when fried, if immersed in ice cold water for five minutes.

Aloo Potol Dalna

Potato and parwar curry

Preparation time: 15 min.
Cooking time: 15 min.
Serves: 2-4

Ingredients:

Potatoes, diced	700 gm
Parwars (*parwal*)	200 gm
Mustard (*sarson*) oil	¾ cup / 150 ml
Cloves (*laung*)	2
Green cardamoms (*choti elaichi*)	2
Cinnamom (*dalchini*) stick	1
Bayleaf (*tej patta*)	1
Black peppercorns (*sabut kali mirch*)	5
Tomatoes, chopped	4 tbsp / 60 gm
Salt to taste	
Turmeric (*haldi*) powder	1 tsp / 5 gm
Red chilli (*lal mirch*) powder	½ tsp / 3 gm
Water	1 cup / 200 ml

Method:

1. Heat the mustard oil in a wok (*kadhai*). Sauté the potatoes and parwars. Drain the excess oil and keep aside.
2. To the same oil, add the cloves, green cardamoms, cinnamon, bayleaf and black peppercorns. Sauté for a few seconds and then add the tomatoes. Cook for 2-3 minutes.
3. Add salt, turmeric powder, red chilli powder, potatoes and parwars. Stir for a few seconds.
4. Add the water and cook till the potatoes are done and the water is absorbed.

Aloo Channa Dalna

Potato and cottage cheese curry

Preparation time: 15 min.
Cooking time: 20 min.
Serves: 2-4

Vegetarian

Ingredients:

Potatoes, diced	200 gm
Cottage cheese (*paneer*), diced	1¼ cups / 250 gm
Oil	½ cup / 100 ml
Cumin seeds (*jeera*)	1 tsp / 5 gm
Turmeric (*haldi*) powder	½ tsp / 3 gm
Coriander (*dhaniya*) powder	1 tsp / 5 gm
Ginger (*adrak*) paste	4 tsp / 20 gm
Red chilli (*lal mirch*) powder	1 tsp / 5 gm
Salt to taste	
Tomatoes, diced	100 gm
Water	1½ cup / 300 ml

Method:

1. Heat 50 ml of oil; sauté the potatoes and cook partially till a skin is formed. Keep aside.
2. In the same oil, sauté the cottage cheese and then dip into water.
3. Heat the remaining oil; add the cumin seeds, turmeric powder, coriander powder, ginger paste, red chilli powder and salt. Sauté for some time.
4. Add the tomatoes and cook till the oil leaves the side of the wok.
5. Mix in the potatoes and cottage cheese and add the water. Cook for 15 minutes or till the curry thickens.
6. Transfer to a serving dish and serve hot.

Aloo Dum

Potato curry

Preparation time: 15 min.
Cooking time: 30 min.
Serves: 2-4

Ingredients:

Potatoes, diced	300 gm
Clarified butter (*ghee*)	2 tsp / 10 gm
Bayleaves (*tej patta*)	2
Cumin seeds (*jeera*)	1 tsp / 5 gm
Tomatoes, diced	100 gm
Turmeric (*haldi*) powder	3 tsp / 15 gm
Salt	1 tsp / 5 gm
Ginger (*adrak*) paste	2 tsp / 10 gm
Yoghurt (*dahi*)	¼ cup / 50 gm
Water	1 cup / 200 ml
Green chillies (*hari mirch*)	2
Green coriander (*hara dhaniya*)	4 tsp / 20 gm

Method:

1. Heat the clarified butter in a wok (*kadhai*); add the bayleaves and cumin seeds. Sauté for some time.
2. Add the tomatoes and sauté along with the turmeric powder, salt and ginger paste. Cook for 1-2 minutes.
3. Add the potatoes and sauté. Pour in the yoghurt, mix well. Then add the water and cook till the potatoes are done.
4. Transfer into a serving dish and serve hot, garnished with green chillies and green coriander.

Aloo Kalo Marich

Potato with black pepper

Preparation time: 40 min.
Cooking time: 5 min.
Serves: 2-4

Ingredients:

Potatoes, boiled, diced	300 gm
Clarified butter (*ghee*)	2 tbsp / 30 gm
Black peppercorns (*sabut kali mirch*), crushed	4 tsp / 20 gm
Salt to taste	

Method:

1. Heat the clarified butter in a wok (*kadhai*); add the potatoes and fry for 2 minutes.
2. Add the black pepper and salt. Toss till the potatoes are coated well with the mixture.
3. Serve hot.

Potato Facts

Potatoes cooked or steamed without their skins lose 14½% of their valuable salts; when cooked in their jackets, they lose only 3%.

Vegetarian

42

Aloo Dimer Dalna

Potato and egg curry

Preparation time: 45 min.
Cooking time: 40 min.
Serves: 2-4

Ingredients:

Potatoes, diced	500 gm
Eggs, hard-boiled	4
Mustard (*sarson*) oil	4 tsp / 20 ml
Onions, chopped	50 gm
Ginger (*adrak*), chopped	2 tsp / 10 gm
Tomatoes, chopped	300 gm
Turmeric (*haldi*) powder	1 tsp / 5 gm
Coriander (*dhaniya*) powder	½ tsp / 3 gm
Red chilli (*lal mirch*) powder	½ tsp / 3 gm
Salt to taste	
Water	1 cup / 200 ml

Method:

1. Heat the mustard oil; add the onions and sauté till lightly browned.
2. Add the ginger, tomatoes and sauté. Mix in all the dry spices and sauté for some time.
3. Add the potatoes, eggs and water. Cook till the gravy thickens and the potatoes are fully cooked.
4. Serve hot.

Bhindi Jhal

Okra curry

Preparation time: 15 min.
Cooking time: 20 min.
Serves: 2-4

Vegetarian

Ingredients:

Okra (*bhindi*)	200 gm
Mustard (*sarson*) oil	2 tbsp / 30 ml
Fresh mustard paste (see p. 6)	2½ tbsp / 40 gm
Salt to taste	
Green chillies (*hari mirch*), slit	4 tsp / 20 gm
Water	¼ cup / 50 ml

Method:

1. Wash the okra; pat dry completely. Cut off the tail and head; slit into half.
2. Heat the mustard oil in a pan and sauté the okra till it is a little soft.
3. Add the mustard paste, salt, green chillies and water.
4. Cook over a medium flame till the okra is done. Serve hot.

Posto Chorchori
Mixed vegetables with poppy seeds

Preparation time: 1 hr.
Cooking time: 30 min.
Serves: 2-4

Vegetarian

Ingredients:

Poppy seeds (*khuskhus*)	¼ cup / 50 gm
Green chillies (*hari mirch*)	2 gm
Broad beans (*sem*), cut into fingers	50 gm
Cauliflower, small florets	50 gm
Aubergines (*baingan*), cut into fingers	60 gm
Radish (*mooli*), cut into fingers	30 gm
Cabbage, chopped	60 gm
Oil	3 tbsp / 45 ml
Turmeric (*haldi*)	2 tsp / 10 gm
Onion seeds (*kalonji*)	1 tsp / 5 gm
Whole red chillies (*sabut lal mirch*)	2 gm
Water	¼ cup / 50 ml
Salt to taste	

Method:

1. Soak the poppy seeds in water and make a paste with green chillies.
2. Heat the oil; add the turmeric, onion seeds and whole red chillies and sauté for half a minute.
3. Add all the vegetables and sauté for about 4 minutes.
4. Add the water, poppy seed paste and salt. Cook till water dries out and the vegetables are cooked.

Sojana Data Posto

Drumsticks with poppy seeds

Preparation time: 20 min.
Cooking time: 25 min.
Serves: 2-4

Ingredients:

Drumsticks (*saijan ki phalli*)	300 gm
Poppy seeds (*khuskhus*)	½ cup / 100 gm
Mustard (*sarson*) oil	2 tbsp / 30 ml
Turmeric (*haldi*) powder	1 tbsp / 15 gm
Salt to taste	
Water	3½ cups / 700 ml

Method:

1. Peel and cut the drumsticks into finger-sized pieces.
2. Wash and soak the poppy seeds in ½ cup of water for half an hour. Grind to a paste.
3. Heat the mustard oil; sauté the drumsticks for a few seconds.
4. Add the turmeric powder, salt, the remaining water and the poppy seed paste.
5. Cook for 20-25 minutes or till the drumsticks are done.

Begun Bhaja
Fried Eggplant

Preparation time: 5 min.
Cooking time: 15 min.
Serves: 2-4

Ingredients:

Eggplant (*baingan*), large, cut into quarters	4
Salt	2 tsp / 10 gm
Turmeric (*haldi*) powder	2 tsp / 10 gm
Mustard (*sarson*) oil	½ cup / 100 ml

Method:

1. Rub the eggplant pieces with salt and turmeric powder. Keep aside for half an hour.
2. Heat the mustard oil in a shallow pan and fry the eggplant pieces till golden brown in colour.
3. Drain the excess oil and serve immediately.

Selecting Eggplants
When buying eggplants, ensure that they are smooth to touch and of light weight. Heaviness indicates that they are overmature with too many seeds.

Bori Diya Palan Saag
Wadi with spinach

Preparation time: 15 min.
Cooking time: 15 min.
Serves: 2-4

Ingredients:

Spinach (*palak*), chopped	250 gm
*Wadi**	10 gm
Oil	2 tbsp / 30 ml
Bayleaves (*tej patta*)	2
Turmeric (*haldi*) powder	1 tsp / 5 gm
Water	¼ cup / 50 ml
Salt to taste	
Sugar	2 tsp / 10 gm

Method:

1. Heat the oil; fry the *wadi* and keep aside.
2. In the same oil, add the bayleaves, turmeric powder and spinach. Fry for 2 minutes.
3. Add the water and *wadi* along with salt to taste and sugar. Cook till the water dries out and the spinach is cooked.
4. Serve hot.

Wadi: Small sun-dried dumplings made with black gram. The black gram is soaked, ground to paste and mixed with spices. Small dumplings of the paste are then spread on plastic sheets and left in the sun till they become dry and hard. Also easily available at all convenience stores.

Vegetarian

Papaya Tarkari
Raw papaya curry

Preparation time: 20 min.
Cooking time: 30 min.
Serves: 2-4

Ingredients:

Raw papaya, diced	300 gm
Oil	2 tbsp / 30 ml
Panch phoran (see p. 6)	2 tsp / 10 gm
Bayleaf (*tej patta*)	1
Turmeric (*haldi*) powder	1 tsp / 5 gm
Ginger (*adrak*) paste	1 tsp / 5 gm
Red chilli powder (*lal mirch*)	1 tsp / 5 gm
Green chillies (*hari mirch*), chopped	2 tsp / 10 gm
Tomatoes, chopped	50 gm
Water	1 cup / 200 ml
Salt to taste	

Method:

1. Heat the oil in a wok (*kadhai*); add the *panch phoran* and bayleaf. Let it crackle for a while.
2. Add the papaya and sauté; add the turmeric powder, ginger paste, red chilli powder, green chillies and tomatoes.
3. Pour in the water and add the salt. Cook till the water dries out and the papaya is cooked.
4. Serve hot.

Bhaja Moong Dal
Broiled green gram

Preparation time: 10 min.
Cooking time: 40 min.
Serves: 2-4

Ingredients:

Split green gram (*moong dal*), washed	200 gm
Oil	2 tbsp / 30 ml
Aniseed (*saunf*)	2 tsp / 10 gm
Cloves (*laung*)	3
Green chillies (*hari mirch*), slit	3
Sugar	1 tsp / 5 gm
Salt to taste	

Method:

1. Broil the split green gram on a griddle (*tawa*) till golden brown.
2. Boil 2 cups of water and cook the split green gram till done.
3. Heat the oil in a small pan; add aniseed, cloves and green chillies. Sauté just for a few seconds and then add to the split green gram.
4. Add the sugar and salt, stir well and serve immediately.

Narkel Chola Dal

Bengal gram with coconut

Preparation time: 10 min.
Cooking time: 45 min.
Serves: 2-4

Vegetarian

Ingredients:

Bengal gram (*chana dal*)	200 gm
Turmeric (*haldi*) powder	1 tsp / 5 gm
Oil	2 tbsp / 30 ml
Aniseed	1 tsp / 5 gm
Cinnamon (*dalchini*) stick	1
Coconut (*nariyal*), fresh, thin small pieces	4 tsp / 20 gm
Salt	1 tsp / 5 gm
Sugar	2 tsp / 10 gm

Method:

1. Boil the Bengal gram with turmeric powder and water till done.
2. Heat the oil and sauté the aniseed and cinnamon. Add the coconut and sauté further for 5 minutes.
3. Add the boiled Bengal gram and then cook for 10 minutes.
4. Mix in the salt and sugar. Serve hot.

Aloo Kopi Dalna

Potato and cauliflower curry

Preparation time: 20 min.
Cooking time: 30 min.
Serves: 2-4

Ingredients:

Potatoes, cut into wedges	200 gm
Cauliflower, cut into florets	100 gm
Oil	¼ cup / 50 ml
Cinnamon (*dalchini*) stick	1
Coriander (*dhaniya*) powder	1 tsp / 5 gm
Red chilli (*lal mirch*) powder	1 tsp / 5 gm
Cumin seed (*jeera*) powder	1 tsp / 5 gm
Ginger (*adrak*) paste	2 tsp / 10 gm
Tomatoes, chopped	¼ cup / 50 gm
Water	2 cups / 400 ml

Method:

1. Heat the oil in a wok (*kadhai*); add the cinnamon stick, coriander powder, red chilli powder and cumin seed powder.
2. Stir and add the potatoes. Cook over a high flame, until they are almost done.
3. Add the ginger paste and tomatoes. Cook for 5 minutes over a medium flame.
4. Add the cauliflower and then the water.
5. Cook over a low flame till the cauliflower is done.

Beguni
Fried eggplant fritters

Preparation time: 15 min.
Cooking time: 10 min.
Serves: 2-4

Ingredients:

Eggplant (*baingan*), large,
   cut into half rounds   4
Gram flour (*besan*)   1 cup / 200 gm
Water   5 tbsp / 75 ml
Refined flour (*maida*)   ¼ cup / 50 gm
Onion seeds (*kalonji*)   1 tsp / 5 gm
Red chilli (*lal mirch*) powder   ½ tsp / 3 gm
Clarified butter (*ghee*) / oil for frying
Baking soda   ½ tsp / 3 gm

Method:

1. Mix together the gramflour, water, refined flour, onion seeds, red chilli powder and the baking soda. Keep aside and allow it to rest for at least two hours.
2. Heat the clarified butter / oil in a wok (*kadhai*); lower the flame.
3. Dip the eggplant pieces in the batter and then fry in the hot oil till they are cooked and golden brown in colour.
4. Drain the excess oil and serve immediately.

Sukhto
Bitter mixed vegetables

Preparation time: 40 min.
Cooking time: 30 min.
Serves: 2-4

Ingredients:

Bitter gourd (*karela*), cut into thin pieces	20 gm
Pumpkin (*sitaphal*), cut into thin pieces	50 gm
Potatoes, cut into thin pieces	50 gm
Brinjals (*baingan*), cut into thin pieces	60 gm
Drumsticks (*saijan ki phali*), cut into thin pieces	20 gm
Banana, raw, cut into thin pieces	60 gm
Dal wadis (see p. 50)	100 gm
Mustard (*sarson*) oil	¼ cup / 50 ml
Panch phoran (see p. 6)	1 tsp / 5 gm
Bayleaf (*tej patta*)	1
Ginger (*adrak*) paste	1 tsp / 5 gm
Mustard (*sarson*) paste (see p. 6)	2 tsp / 10 gm
Sugar	2 tsp / 10 gm
Water	½ cup / 100 ml
Salt	1 tsp / 5 gm
Milk	1 tbsp / 15 ml

Method:

1. Deep-fry the *dal wadis* until golden brown and keep aside.
2. Heat the oil; add the *panch phoran* and bayleaf. Sauté for a few seconds. Add the bitter gourd, pumpkin, potatoes, brinjals, drumsticks and

bananas and cook until they become tender and a little brown in colour.

3. Add the ginger paste, mustard paste, sugar and water. Cook covered for 20 minutes over a medium flame.

4. Just before serving, heat through, stir in the milk and add the *dal wadis*. Cook just for a minute. Remove from the flame, transfer into a serving dish and serve hot. This dish is usually accompanied with steamed rice.

Long Lasting

*Preserve bitter gourd (**karela**) by drying it.*
Cut into thin slices and sun-dry.
Store in airtight containers.

Posto Bora
Poppy seed patties

Preparation time: 40 min.
Cooking time: 15 min.
Serves: 2-4

Vegetarian

Ingredients:

Poppy seeds (*khuskhus*)	300 gm
Potatoes, boiled, mashed	100 gm
Gram flour (*besan*)	¼ cup / 50 gm
Green chillies (*hari mirch*)	2 tbsp / 30 gm
Onions, chopped	2 tbsp / 30 gm
Salt to taste	
Oil	½ cup / 100 ml

Method:

1. Soak the poppy seeds in double the quantity of water for 2 hours and keep aside. Grind to a paste.
2. Mix the potatoes with the gram flour, green chillies and onions. Add the seasoning and poppy seed paste.
3. Mix all the ingredients together and make 4 balls. Flatten the balls and keep aside.
4. Heat the oil in a pan and shallow-fry the flattened balls till golden brown.
5. Serve hot with tamarind chutney.

Kathal Aloo Tarkari
Jackfruit and potato curry

Preparation time: 40 min.
Cooking time: 40 min.
Serves: 2-4

Ingredients:

Jackfruit (*kathal*), diced	300 gm
Potatoes, diced	150 gm
Oil	½ cup / 100 ml
Onions, chopped	50 gm
Ginger-garlic (*adrak-lasan*) paste	2 tsp / 10 gm
Turmeric (*haldi*) powder	1 tsp / 5 gm
Coriander (*dhaniya*) powder	1 tsp / 5 gm
Red chilli (*lal mirch*) powder	1 tsp / 5 gm
Cumin seed (*jeera*) powder	1 tsp / 5 gm
Tomatoes, chopped	50 gm
Salt to taste	
Water	1½ cups / 300 ml

Method:

1. Heat the oil in a wok (*kadhai*); add the jackfruit and potatoes and sauté for 10-12 minutes and keep aside.
2. In the same oil, add the onions, ginger-garlic paste and the dry spices. Sauté for 5 minutes.
3. Add the tomatoes and cook till the oil separates from the sides of the wok (*kadhai*).
4. Add the jackfruit, potatoes, salt and water. Cook till the vegetables are tender.

Neem Begun

Brinjals with tender neem leaves

Preparation time: 15 min.
Cooking time: 30 min.
Serves: 2-4

I n g r e d i e n t s :

Tender neem leaves	50 gm
Brinjals (*baingan*), diced	150 gm
Salt	2 tsp / 10 gm
Turmeric (*haldi*) powder	1 tsp / 5 gm
Mustard (*sarson*) oil	¼ cup / 50 ml

M e t h o d :

1. Marinate the brinjals with the salt and turmeric powder for 15 minutes.
2. Heat the oil in a wok (*kadhai*); deep-fry the marinated pieces till crisp. Keep aside.
3. In the same oil, deep-fry the neem leaves. Keep aside.
4. Mix the two together and serve with steamed rice and clarified butter.

Vegetarian

Kacha Kala Jhol

Raw banana curry

Preparation time: 30 min.
Cooking time: 40 min.
Serves: 2-4

Ingredients:

Raw banana, diced	50 gm
Potatoes, diced	50 gm
Cauliflower (*phool gobi*)	40 gm
Brinjal (*baingan*)	60 gm
Mustard (*sarson*) oil	4 tsp / 20 ml
Panch phoran (see p. 6)	1 tsp / 5 gm
Turmeric (*haldi*) powder	½ tsp / 3 gm
Ginger (*adrak*) paste	1 tsp / 5 gm
Salt to taste	
Water	1½ cups / 300 ml

Method:

1. Heat the mustard oil in a wok (*kadhai*); add the *panch phoran*. Then add the potatoes and sauté for a while. Add the raw bananas, cauliflower and brinjals.

2. Add the turmeric powder, ginger paste, salt and water. Cook till the vegetables are done.

3. Serve hot.

Aloo Posto
Potato with poppy seeds

Ingredients:

Potatoes, diced	200 gm
Poppy seeds (*khuskhus*)	¼ cup / 50 gm
Mustard (*sarson*) oil	2 tbsp / 30 ml
Turmeric (*haldi*) powder	1 tsp / 5 gm
Salt	2 tsp / 10 gm
Water	2 cups / 400 ml
Green chillies (*hari mirch*), chopped	2 tsp / 10 gm

Method:

1. Boil the poppy seeds in double the quantity of water; grind into a paste. Keep aside.
2. Heat the mustard oil in a wok (*kadhai*) and sauté the potatoes for 3-4 minutes.
3. Add the poppy seed paste, turmeric powder, salt and water. Cook till the potatoes are done.
4. Add the green chillies and serve immediately.

Vegetarian

Chira Bhaja
Fried pressed rice

Preparation time: 30 min.
Cooking time: 10 min.
Serves: 2-4

Ingredients:

Pressed rice (*chidwa*)	200 gm
Oil for frying	
Peanuts (*moongphalli*)	¼ cup / 50 gm
Potatoes, julienned	¼ cup / 50 gm
Salt	1 tbsp / 15 gm
Black peppercorns (*sabut kali mirch*), crushed	1 tsp / 5 gm

Method:

1. Heat the oil in a wok (*kadhai*); fry the pressed rice, peanuts and potatoes separately. Drain the excess oil.
2. In a big mixing bowl, combine all the ingredients.
3. Add the salt and black pepper; mix gently till the whole mixture is seasoned.
4. This can be served hot or at room temperature.

Kopi Shingara

Deep-fried, cauliflower stuffed savoury patty

Preparation time: 40 min.
Cooking time: 20 min.
Portions: 6

Ingredients:

Cauliflower (*phool gobi*), cut into florets	250 gm
Refined flour (*maida*)	1 ¼ cup / 250 gm
Clarified butter (*ghee*)	¼ cup / 50 gm
Onion seeds (*kalonji*)	1 tsp / 5 gm
Oil for frying	
Cumin seeds (*jeera*)	1 tsp / 5 gm
Mango powder (*amchur*)	1 tsp / 5 gm
Green chillies (*hari mirch*), chopped	1 tsp / 5 gm
Salt	2 tsp / 10 gm
Turmeric (*haldi*) powder	½ tsp / 3 gm

Method:

1. Mix together the refined flour, clarified butter and onion seeds. Add just enough water and knead into a stiff dough. Keep aside.
2. Heat the oil; deep-fry the cauliflower. Drain the excess oil. Keep aside to cool. Chop into small pieces.
3. Heat the clarified butter and sauté the cumin seeds. Add the mango powder, green chillies, salt, turmeric powder and cauliflower. Mix well and remove from the flame.
4. Make small, lemon-sized balls of the dough. Roll out each ball into discs, 6″-8″ in diameter.
5. Cut each disc into half, put ½ tbsp of the cauliflower filling in the middle of one half disc.

Fold the disc into a triangular shape, enclosing the filling. Pinch the loose edges with your forefinger and thumb to seal. Likewise, prepare all the *samosas*.

6. Reheat the oil in a wok (*kadhai*) and fry the samosas over a medium flame, till they are golden brown in colour. Drain the excess oil and serve immediately.

Better Buy
When buying cauliflower, ensure that it is round, white and compact with closely knit flowers.

Chingri Maacher Cutlets

Prawn cutlets

Preparation time: 20 min.
Cooking time: 10 min.
Serves: 2-4

Ingredients:

Prawns, cleaned, deveined, finely chopped	400 gm
Cumin seeds (*jeera*)	1 tsp / 5 gm
Whole red chillies (*sabut lal mirch*)	1 tsp / 5 gm
Green cardamoms (*choti elaichi*), powdered	½ tsp / 3 gm
Ginger (*adrak*), chopped	4 tsp / 20 gm
Green chillies (*hari mirch*), chopped	1 tbsp / 15 gm
Salt to taste	
Eggs, whisked	2
Breadcrumbs	½ cup / 100 gm
Oil for deep-frying	

Method:

1. Broil the cumin seeds, whole red chillies and green cardamoms. Grind to a powder and set aside.
2. To the prawns, add ginger, green chillies and salt. Add the powdered mixture and mix well.
3. Shape the mixture into small even rounds, flatten and keep aside.
4. Heat the oil; dip each round in the egg, coat with breadcrumbs and deep-fry until golden brown in colour.
5. Serve hot.

Nimki
Flour crispies

Preparation time: 15 min.
Cooking time: 10 min.
Serves: 2-4

Ingredients:

Refined flour (*maida*)	250 gm
Clarified butter (*ghee*)	2 tbsp / 30 gm
Salt	2 tsp / 10 gm
Water	4 tbsp / 60 ml
Onion seeds (*kalonji*)	4 tsp / 20 gm
Oil for frying	

Method:

1. Mix together the refined flour, clarified butter and salt.
2. Add the onion seeds and water; knead into a firm dough.
3. Divide the dough into small equal-sized balls.
4. Flatten the balls and roll them out into discs. Dust flour on both sides of the discs and then fold each into quarters (will be triangular in shape).
5. Heat the oil in a wok (*kadhai*); fry the quarters, over a medium flame till crisp and golden in colour. Drain the excess oil.
6. Store in an airtight container; these can last upto two weeks.

Jhal Muri
Seasoned puffed rice

Preparation time: 15 min.
Serves: 2-4

Ingredients:

Puffed rice (*murmura*)	250 gm
Onion, finely chopped	2 tbsp / 30 gm
Potato, boiled, peeled, finely chopped	2 tbsp / 30 gm
Tomatoes, finely chopped	2 tbsp / 30 gm
Cucumber, finely chopped	2 tbsp / 30 gm
Ginger (*adrak*), finely chopped	2 tsp / 10 gm
Green chillies (*hari mirch*), finely chopped	4 tsp / 20 gm
Peanuts (*moongphalli*), fried	2 tbsp / 30 gm
Sprouted black gram (*kala chana*), soaked, drained	2 tsp / 10 gm
Mustard (*sarson*) oil	4 tsp / 20 ml
Salt	1 tsp / 5 gm

Method:

1. Combine all the ingredients except the mustard oil and salt. Mix gently with a fork.
2. Now add the mustard oil and salt. Mix gently again.
3. Serve as a snack at tea-time.

Ghee Bhat
Rice with clarified butter

Preparation time: 10 min.
Cooking time: 30 min.
Serves: 2-4

Ingredients:

Basmati rice	200 gm
Clarified butter (*ghee*)	3¼ tbsp / 50 gm
Cloves (*laung*)	2
Cinnamon (*dalchini*)	1
Bayleaf (*tej patta*)	1
Black peppercorns (*sabut kali mirch*)	5
Water	2 cups / 400 ml
Salt	1 tsp / 5 gm

Method:

1. Clean, wash and soak the rice for 2 hours. Drain the water and keep aside.
2. Heat the clarified butter; sauté the cloves, cinnamon, bayleaf and black peppercorns for a few seconds.
3. Add the rice and sauté for 1 minute. Immediately add the water and salt.
4. Cook until the rice is done and the water gets absorbed. Serve hot.

Channa pulao

Soft cottage cheese pilaf

Preparation time: 20 min.
Cooking time: 10 min.
Serves: 2-4

Ingredients:

Basmati rice	250 gm
Soft cottage cheese (*paneer*)	¼ cup / 50 gm
Clarified butter (*ghee*)	2 tbsp / 30 gm
Cloves (*laung*)	2
Green cardamoms (*choti elaichi*)	2
Cinnamon (*dalchini*)	1
Bayleaf (*tej patta*)	1
Saffron (*kesar*), soaked in 2 tsp milk	a pinch
Salt to taste	
Water, hot	3 cups / 600 ml

Method:

1. Clean, wash and soak the rice in water for 2 hours. Drain the water; spread out the rice and leave to dry.
2. Heat the clarified butter; add the cloves, green cardamoms, cinnamon, bayleaf and soft cottage cheese.
3. Cook till the cottage cheese is slightly golden brown in colour.
4. Add the rice, saffron-milk, salt and water. Cover and cook on a medium flame, till the rice is done and the water gets absorbed. Serve hot.

Luchi
Deep-fried flour bread

Preparation time: 20 min.
Cooking time: 10 min.
Serves: 2-4

Ingredients:

Refined flour (*maida*)	500 gm
Clarified butter (*ghee*)	¼ cup / 50 gm
Clarified butter (*ghee*) to fry	
Salt	½ tsp / 3 gm
Water	½ cup / 100 ml

Method:

1. Make a stiff dough with flour, clarified butter and water. Keep aside for 2 hours.
2. Separate the dough into small round lemon-sized balls.
3. Roll out the balls into flat discs, about 4″ in diameter.
4. Heat the clarified butter for frying; deep-fry the discs till golden brown in colour.
5. Serve hot as an accompaniment.

Motor Chuti Kachori

Green pea patties

Preparation time: 45 min.
Cooking time: 30 min.
Serves: 2-4

Ingredients:

Green peas, shelled	500 gm
Cumin seeds (*jeera*)	2 tbsp / 30 gm
Whole red chillies (*sabut lal mirch*)	4 tsp / 20 gm
Green cardamoms (*choti elaichi*)	2 tsp / 10 gm
Clarified butter (*ghee*)	2 tbsp / 30 gm
Salt to taste	
Red chilli (*lal mirch*) powder	2 tbsp / 30 gm
Refined flour (*maida*)	1½ cups / 300 gm
Water	4½ tbsp / 70 ml
Clarified butter (*ghee*)	2 tbsp / 30 gm
Oil / clarified butter (*ghee*) for frying	

Method:

1. Grind the green peas into a paste.
2. Broil the cumin seeds, whole red chillies and green cardamoms and then powder them. Keep aside.
3. Heat the clarified butter; cook the green pea paste with salt, red chilli powder and the broiled powder. Keep the stuffing aside.
4. Make a stiff dough by using flour, water and clarified butter. Keep the dough for 2 hours in the fridge.
5. Divide the dough into equal-sized balls. Take each ball, make a well in the middle, add the stuffing and cover it. Shape like small patties and deep-fry till golden. Serve hot.

Tomato Khajoor Chutney

Tomato and date chutney

Preparation time: 30 min.
Cooking time: 30 min.

Ingredients:

Tomatoes, chopped	1kg
Dates (*khajur*), deseeded	¼ cup / 50 gm
Oil	2 tsp / 10 ml
Mustard seeds (*rai*)	1 tsp / 5 gm
Dry red chillies (*sookhi lal mirch*)	2
Sugar	½ cup / 100 gm
Salt to taste	

Method:

1. Heat the oil; add the mustard seeds and dry red chillies. Sauté for a few seconds, till the mustard seeds crackle.
2. Add the tomatoes and cook for 15 minutes. Add the sugar and salt; stir till the sugar dissolves completely.
3. Cook till the mixture obtains a thick consistency. Mix in the dates in the end.
4. Serve after it cools. When refrigerated this chutney can stay up to 2-3 days.

(Photograph on page 3, right dish)

Papaya Chutney

Preparation time: 15 min.
Cooking time: 15 min.
Serves: 2-4

Ingredients:

Raw papaya, diced	300 gm
Oil	4 tsp / 20 ml
Panch phoran (see p. 6)	1 tsp / 5 gm
Sugar	½ cup / 100 gm
Water	¼ cup / 50 ml
Raisins (*kishmish*)	2 tbsp / 30 gm
Lemon (*nimbu*) juice	¼ cup / 50 ml

Method:

1. Heat the oil in a wok (*kadhai*); add the *panch phoran* and sauté for a few seconds.
2. Add the raw papaya and sauté for 4 minutes. Add the sugar, water and raisins and cook till the papaya is done and the water is nearly dried.
3. Pour in the lemon juice, mix well and remove from the flame.
4. Serve chilled.

(Photograph on page 3, left dish)

Rosgolla

Cottage cheese dumplings in sugar syrup

Preparation time: I hr.
Cooking time: 45 min.
Serves: 2-4

Ingredients:

Milk	7½ cups / 1.5 lt
Lemon (*nimbu*) juice	3 tsp / 15 ml
Semolina (*suji*)	2 tsp / 10 gm
Water	5 cups / 1 lt
Sugar	1½ cups / 300 gm
Rose water (*gulab jal*)	2 tsp / 10 ml

Method:

1. Bring the milk to a boil; add the lemon juice to make the milk curdle.
2. Pass the curdled milk through a muslin cloth. Tie the ends of the cloth and let it hang for 6 hours.
3. When all the whey is drained from the cottage cheese, add the semolina and then knead well to make a smooth dough.
4. Break the dough and shape into small lemon-sized, round balls.
5. Boil the water; add the sugar and rose water. Cook until it becomes a thick syrup.
6. Carefully slide the balls into the syrup and cook until they become light and fluffy and start floating.
7. Remove from the flame and put aside to cool. Serve chilled.

Sandesh

Creamy cheese fudge

Preparation time: 40 min.
Cooking time: 45 min.
Serves: 2-4

Ingredients:

Soft cottage cheese (*channa*)	500 gm
Sugar	7 ½ tbsp / 80 gm
Jaggery (*gur*)	7 ½ tbsp / 80 gm

Method:

1. Prepare the soft cottage cheese (see p. 7); hang it in a cloth to drain the water.
2. Divide the cottage cheese into two parts; mix sugar into one portion and jaggery into the other.
3. Cook both the mixtures separately till they become dry and powdery. Keep aside to cool.
4. Combine both the mixtures when they cool and mix well. Make small round balls out of it.
5. Put the balls in small fudge moulds and press so that the ball takes the shape of the mould. Serve cold. Can be kept refrigerated for up to 4 days.

Desserts

Rasmalai

Cottage cheese patties in sweetened milk

Preparation time: 30 min.
Cooking time: 30 min.
Serves: 2-4

Ingredients:

Soft cottage cheese (*channa*), (see p. 7)	500 gm
Semolina (*suji*)	2 tsp / 10 gm
Sugar	10 cups / 2 kg
Water	5 cups / 1 lt
Milk	15 cups / 3 lt
Cardamom (*elaichi*) powder	2 tsp /10 gm
Pistachios (*pista*), slivered	4 tsp / 20 gm

Method:

1. Knead the cottage cheese with the semolina well, till it is light and fluffy. Divide and shape into small round lemon-sized balls.
2. Make a thick sugar syrup with 1 lt water. Keep aside.
3. Flatten the balls to make patties and then poach (see p. 93) them in the thick syrup for 15 minutes.
4. Bring the milk to a boil and cook until it is reduced to three-quarters of the original quantity (about 20 minutes). Add the remaining sugar and cardamom powder. Stir till the sugar dissolves completely.
5. Add the poached patties to the hot milk. Remove from the flame and cool.
6. Serve chilled, garnished with pistachios.

Desserts

Lavang Latika
Coconut-stuffed flour crispies

Preparation time: 2 hr.
Cooking time: I hr.
Serves: 2-4

Ingredients:

For the dough

Flour (*maida*)	230 gm
Clarified butter (*ghee*)	1 cup / 100 gm
Milk, warm	2 tsp / 10 ml
Baking powder	1 tsp / 5 gm
Water	2 tsp / 10 ml

For the filling

Coconut (*nariyal*), grated	5½ tbsp / 80 gm
Raisins (*kishmish*)	10-20
Green cardamoms (*choti elaichi*), crushed	2
Sugar	¼ cup / 50 gm
Clarified butter (*ghee*) for frying	
Cloves (*laung*), for securing	10-12

For the syrup

Sugar	1¼ cup / 250 gm
Water	2 cups / 400 ml

Method:

1. Make a stiff dough with flour, clarified butter, warm milk, baking powder and water. Let the dough lie for at least 2 hours.
2. Make the filling by mixing the coconut, raisins, sugar and green cardamoms together.
3. Make the sugar syrup and keep aside.
4. Divide the dough into small rectangular shapes. Put the filling mixture in the middle and fold to make small parcels.
5. Secure with a clove and deep-fry over very low heat till golden brown. Drain excess oil, transfer to the pan with sugar syrup. Remove with a slotted spoon and refrigerate. Serve chilled.

Suggested Menus

Non-vegetarian
Doi Maach (*Fish with yoghurt*) — 8
Murgi Kalia (*Chicken curry*) — 34

or

Vegetarian
Aloo Channa Dalna — 40
(*Potato and cottage cheese curry*)
Begun Bhaja (*Fried eggplant*) — 48

Accompaniments
Ghee Bhat (*Rice with clarified butter*) — 76
Luchi (*Deep-fried flour bread*) — 78

Dessert
Rosgolla — 84
(*Cottage cheese dumplings in sugar syrup*)

Non-vegetarian
Saser Maach Kala Pata Dia — 18
(*Fish wrapped in banana leaves*)
Potoler Dhorma (*Stuffed parwars*) — 14

or

Vegetarian
Sukhto (*Bitter mixed vegetables*) — 58
Narkel Chola Dal — 54
(*Bengal gram with coconut*)

Accompaniments
Channa Pulao (*Soft cottage cheese pilaf*) — 77
Motor Chuti Kachori — 80
(*Green pea patties*)

Dessert
Sandesh (*Creamy cheese fudge*) — 86

Glossary of Cooking Terms

Broil — Dry roast the food items in a heavy-bottomed pan over low heat without using oil or water.

Poach — Gently cook food items in water or flavoured liquid at a temperature just below boiling point.

Marinade — A seasoned mixture of oil, vinegar, lemon juice, etc. in which meat, poultry or fish is left for some time to soften its fibres and add flavour to it.

Stir-fry — Cook over high heat with oil or any other liquid, stirring briskly.

Stew — Cook in liquid which is at least 8 times the amount of food over medium heat.

Steam — Cook by heat or steam. Generally items to be steamed are put in a perforated container and put over boiling water.

Index

ISBN: 81-7436-128-6

© **Roli Books Pvt. Ltd. 2000**
Lustre Press Pvt. Ltd.

Second impression 2002
M-75, Greater Kailash-II Market,
New Delhi-110 048, INDIA
Phones: (011) 6442271, 6462782, 6460886
Fax: (011) 6467185, E-mail: roli@vsnl.com
Website: rolibooks.com

Photographs: Dheeraj Paul

Printed and bound in Singapore